Oregon
Wildflowers

A children's
field guide to
the state's most
common flowers

Interpreting the Great Outdoors

Text by Beverly Magley, Illustrations by DD Dowden

For Blake and Bethany,
with love,
  Aunt Bevy

Interpreting the Great Outdoors

Nature's wonders, such as the wildflowers, are certainly remarkable, but unfortunately many people—especially young people—know little about them. That's one reason Falcon Press has launched this series of books called Interpreting the Great Outdoors.

Other books in the series include *The Tree Giants: The Story of the Redwoods, the World's Largest Trees; The Fire Mountains: The Story of the Cascade Volcanoes; California Wildflowers;* and *Arizona Wildflowers.*

To get extra copies of this book or others in the Interpreting the Great Outdoors series, write to Falcon Press, P.O. Box 1718, Helena, MT 59624. Or call toll-free 1-800-582-2665. Falcon Press publishes and distributes a wide variety of books and calendars, so be sure to ask for our free catalog.

Botanical consultant—Cascade Anderson Geller

Design, illustrations, editing, typesetting, and other prepress work by Falcon Press, Helena, Montana. Printed in Hong Kong.

Library of Congress Number 91-77419
ISBN 1-56044-035-X

Contents

Introduction

Wildflowers can be fragile or as tough as nails. They can grow on the coldest, highest mountain or underwater in a swamp, along a busy footpath or in the hot, dry desert. They can endure weather that sends us people running for cover and then lift their cheerful blossoms to the sun the very next day.

Flowering plants have existed for about 120 million years. They evolved when dinosaurs roamed the earth. They are unique because each of their seeds has a protective, nourishing shell that helps the seed to survive. And survival is the primary goal of every living thing.

Wildflowers entice visitors with their nectar, and the nectar-eaters then pollinate the blossoms so they can produce seeds. A nice trade! So when you see an ant crawling inside a flower or watch a hummingbird sipping nectar, remember they are essential to the survival of flowers. In addition to providing food, flowers may provide shelter for insects and other little creatures.

Oregon provides many different kinds of homes for wildflowers. High mountains create different living conditions than dry deserts; seashores differ from freshwater streams. Most flowers are adapted to specific conditions, but a few flowering plants are so versatile they can live almost anywhere.

Please don't pick wildflowers. If you pick a flower it dies. If you leave it blooming in its home, the blossom will eventually scatter seeds that will provide another year of beautiful wildflowers you can come back to enjoy.

Wildflower, when I look on thee
All that's wild and sweet in me
Soars free

Sanna Porte Kiesling

Pacific Coast

Waves pound the jagged rocks and steep bluffs along the shore. Calm tidal pools and white beaches beckon beachcombers. Sand dunes shift up against thick forests of pines, oaks, maples, alders, and dogwoods.

This is the coastal world of Oregon—salty, wet, and exciting. Plants that grow here must be able to withstand extreme winds or weeks of fog and rain. Some flowers hug the ground in sheltered sand dunes while others take refuge in thickets. Many have roots that extend deep into the ground, both for stability and to find water. You can find wildflowers any month of the year here, but especially between January and October.

Scotch Broom

other name: Common Broom
height: up to 10 feet
season: April to June

Early-day housekeepers in Scotland and other European countries swept their floors with brooms made of these branches. They brought the plant with them when they came to America. Today the bright golden flowers of this big shrub adorn many Oregon bluffs and islands. The seedpods can be pickled and eaten, or roasted to make a coffee substitute.

*Cytisus
scoparius*

Sea Rocket

other name: Oval Searocket
height: 6 to 20 inches
season: July to September

The purplish flower with its bright yellow center eventually fades to white, and the seedpod looks like a miniature rocket ready to launch into the sky. Waxy, swollen leaves are a bluish green, with wavy edges or big coarse teeth. The leaves and young seedpods add a spicy hot tang to salads.

*Cakile
edentula*

Coast Manroot

other name: Bigroot
height: stems up to 20 feet long
season: March to June

Some people think this underground tuber is shaped like a tiny man with little arms and legs. Some roots grow to be as heavy as twenty pounds—the size of a toddler! Above ground, the bell-like flower yields a round, inedible fruit that is either smooth or has soft little spines.

*Marah
oreganus*

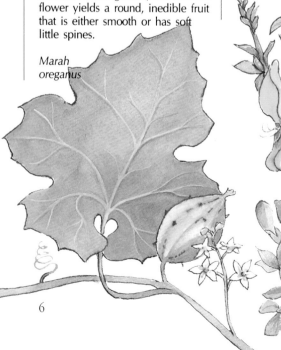

Horsetail

other names: Scouring Rush,
    Mare's Tail, Shavegrass
height: 6 inches to 5 feet
season: March to May

When dinosaurs lived, this plant grew ninety feet tall! The common name horsetail comes from the plant's Latin name: *equus*, which means horse, and *seta*, which means bristle. Indians used the rough stems to polish pipes, bows, and arrows. You can make a whistle from a piece of the hollow, leafless stem.

Equisetum hyemale L.

Pacific Silverweed

other names: Goosegrass,
    Cinquefoil, Fivefingers
height: a low creeper, flower
    stalks may reach
    1 foot high
season: May to July

Silvery hairs on the undersides of the leaves give this plant one of its names. Each plant sends out runners that take root and grow into new plants. The roots can be boiled or roasted, and they taste a bit like parsnips. Pacific coast Indians are said to have eaten the root steamed and dipped in whale oil.

Potentilla pacifica

Beach Pea

other names: Sea Pea,
    Seashore Peavine
height: 8 to 24 inches
season: May to September

Beach peas grow in dense colonies on sand dunes and beaches. The flowers are similar to those of the garden-variety sweet pea. They may be pink, light blue, or even dark purple. After blossoming, the 2.5-inch-long seedpods stick up into the air. Nootka Indians wove the sweet-smelling flowers into their grass baskets.

Lathyrus japonicus

7

Roadsides and Disturbed Areas

People have a way of disrupting natural plant communities. We bulldoze roads, dig ditches, build railroads, and make trails. We build homes and plant garden flowers that go to seed and sprout up somewhere else. Sometimes we accidentally or intentionally set fires that burn an are

Nature, too, can disturb plant habitat, through lightning fires, rock slides, or floods.

All these disturbances create unique conditions that many plants find too harsh. But some are able to grow and flourish. Although we might think of them as weeds, they are an important p of nature because they stabilize the soil with their roots, add needed nutrients, and prepare the way for grasses, shrubs, and trees to grow someday.

Next time you see a tall mullein or feathery Queen Anne's lace growing alongside the road, remember its essential role of healing the land.

Red Clover

other name: Trefoil
height: 1 to 3 feet
season: June to August

Bumblebees and hummingbirds love the red clover's sweet nectar. You might, too—try sucking on the pinkish florets for a yummy taste. Bears, beavers, rabbits, and raccoons also love the flavor. At night, the leaflets fold down to protect the sensitive surfaces from the cold air.

Trifolium pratense

Henbit

other name: Dead Nettle
height: 3 to 6 inches
season: March to August

This small plant has unusual habits. Its first flowers often never open and simply fertilize themselves. Later blossoms open to reveal a bright reddish purple color. The common name dead nettle refers to this nettle's inability to sting.

Lamium amplexicaule

Dandelion

other name: Blowball
height: 2 to 12 inches
season: year-round

Hungry bumblebees love the nectar of dandelions. The plant's name comes from the French words *dent de lion,* which mean teeth of the lion. Look for the five little teeth at the outside edge of each yellow floret, and notice the jagged, toothlike leaves. The dandelion may be the world's most widespread and useful flower. The leaves, roots, and flowers are edible and contain calcium and vitamins. Some people remove warts by putting the milky latex stem juice on them.

Taraxacum officinale

Shepherd's Purs

other name: Mother's Heart
height: 12 inches
season: year-round

The sticky little heart-shaped seedpo look like the tiny purses or bags that shepherds and pasto once carried. When it's wet outside, inse often get stuck to the seedpods an die, providir nourishment for the ne seedling

Capse bursa-pasto

Fireweed

other names: Tall Willowherb,
Blooming Sally
height: 2 to 6 feet
season: June to September

Fireweed is often the first plant to grow in an area devastated by a forest fire. It helps enrich the burned area so that other plants can move back in. The flower blooms from the bottom up, so you may see seedpods, flowers, and buds on one plant. The seeds can be carried long distances by their little parachute-like hairs.

Epilobium angustifolium

Blue Sailor

other names: Bachelor Button,
Chicory
height: up to 6 inches
season: March to October

Try a science experiment with this flower: Knock gently on an anthill with a stick until the ants come scurrying out. Hold the blue sailor blossom near the ants and watch them shoot up formic acid to defend their mound. The blossom acts like natural litmus paper and turns pink where it's hit by the acid. Roasted roots can be mixed with coffee to make a tasty hot drink.

Cichorium intybus

Mullein

other names: Witch's Candle,
Flannel Plant, American
Velvet Plant, Torch
Flower
height: 2 to 7 feet
season: June to August

The word mullein comes from *moleyne*, a Middle English word for soft. Hummingbirds line their little nests with soft hairs from the leaves. In olden times, the tall flower spike was dipped in tallow and burned as a torch for celebrations. It's fun to throw a dried stalk like a javelin.

Verbascum thapsus

9

Oxeye Daisy

other name: Marguerite
height: 1 to 2 feet
season: May to October

English people called this flower a "day's eye" because it opens each day and closes at night. The outer white rays surround a yellow center. Look through a magnifying glass for a closeup of the hundreds of tiny yellow tubular florets packed into the center. In Italy, the young leaves are eaten in salads.

Chrysanthemum leucanthemum

Foxglove

other names: Folk's Glove,
Fairy's Glove
height: 2 to 7 feet
season: June to July

Flared, tube-shaped flowers hang in a spire around the stem. The Irish and English called this folk's glove or fairy's glove. Maybe the tiny maroon or red speckles are where fairies touched the plant. Foxglove has very poisonous leaves and is well known for its use as a heart medicine.

Digitalis purpurea

Lupine

other name: Bluebonnet
height: 8 to 30 inches
season: April to May

Lupinus is the Latin word for wolf. The lupine got its name because early people mistakenly thought the plant robbed nutrients from the soil like a wolf robbed sheep from a shepherd. In fact, just the opposite is true. Lupines actually enrich poor soils with special nitrogen-stabilizing bacteria attached to their roots. Blossom colors range from white to pink to blue to purple.

Lupinus spp.

Queen Anne's Lace

other names: Wild Carrot,
    Bird's Nest
height: 1 to 4 feet
season: May to September

In the 1700s, Queen Anne of England wore this pretty ancestor of the garden carrot instead of cloth lace. The central, pinkish flower could be a drop of her blood where she pricked her finger sewing the flower to her collar. Put the stem of a cut flower in food coloring and water to dye the blossom. Then press and dry the blossom to make a pretty snowflake-like holiday ornament.

Daucus carota

Butter and Eggs

other name: Toadflax
height: 1 to 2 feet
season: June to July

The flower is gold and yellow, like an egg yolk in a pan of butter. The other common name is toadflax. Squeeze a blossom gently from the sides and watch it open up like a toad's mouth. The juice from the leaves may stop your mosquito bites from itching.

Linaria vulgaris

Bull Thistle

other name: Lightning Plant
height: 2 to 3 feet
season: June to October

A legend tells why a thistle is the national emblem of Scotland. One night long ago, the Danes invaded Scotland and took off their boots to sneak up on a village. One soldier stepped on a thistle and yelled in pain, and the villagers awoke in time to defend themselves and their country.

*Cirsium
vulgare*

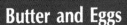

11

Marshes, Ponds & Wetlands

Pull on your rubber boots to look for these flowers. Most plants can't live in standing or moving water, but a few have evolved so that they can grow with their roots submerged in water while their leaves float on top. Other plants aren't able to get enough nutrients from the soil and have learned to digest insects. Whatever their ways of adapting, the blossoms are sure to be beautiful, interesting, or both.

Skunk Cabbage

other name: Yellow Arum
height: 1 to 2 feet
season: April to July

The poisonous leaf covering, called a spathe, smells a bit skunky when injured. The smell attracts such pollinators as beetles, who like stinky, rotting things. Little ridges on the roots pull the plant close to the ground each spring to keep the leaves and flower buds away from cold winds. The unusual knob of flowers is called a spadix.

Lysichitum americanum

Umbrella Plant

other names: Shield Leaf, Indian Rhubarb
height: 2 to 6 feet
season: April to June

Round clusters of pink or white flowers form a miniature umbrella at the end of the stalk. The big round leaves with their jagged teeth can be more than a foot wide.

Peltiphyllum peltatum

Pitcher Plant

other names: Cobra Lily, Indian Cup
height: up to 3 feet
season: June to August

This plant actually eats insects! Sweet nectar entices insects to alight on the mouth of the blossom. The bug gets trapped there by tiny barbed hairs, and then it falls into the pitcher-shaped blossom. Plant fluids digest the unlucky critter.

Darlingtonia californica

Cattail

other names: none
height: 4 to 8 feet
season: June to November

Ever had a cattail pancake? Indians used every part of this plant. The roots are edible, and the pollen can be used like flour to make pancakes, breads, or cakes. The leaves can be woven into baskets. The downy seeds are good insulation and make good pillow stuffing or absorbent padding for diapers.

Typha latifolia

Yellow Water Lily

other names: Spatterdock,
    Indian Pond Lily
height: 1 to 3 inches above
    the water
season: April to September

The heart-shaped leaves often float on the surface of a calm pond, while the yellow cup-shaped flowers reach just above the water's surface. To survive in water, the plant brings air down the hollow stems of young leaves and then returns it up the stems of older leaves. Indians roasted the seeds like popcorn or ground them into flour for bread.

Nuphar polysepala

American Brooklime

other name: Speedwell
height: 6 to 12 inches high,
    stems up to 3 feet
season: May to August

Purple lines, or pathfinders, direct insects to the nectar in these tiny violet blossoms. This plant likes to grow in mud or the calm water of little brooks. It's also called speedwell because it was used to help wounds heal quickly.

Veronica americana

Streams and Riverbanks

Flowing water and muddy banks provide abundant moisture for many brightly colored flowers that like to grow alongside rivers and streams. Animals come to drink and sample the tasty flowers and leaves.

When you go out to look for these flowers, maybe you can take a picnic, or float along the banks in a boat.

Shooting Star

other names: Peacock Flower,
  Bird's Bill, Sailor Cap,
  Mosquito Bill
height: 6 to 16 inches
season: May to July

Perhaps one really windy day these flowers turned inside out and decided to stay that way. Now they appear to shoot through the sky like small pink stars aimed at the earth.

Monkeyflower

other name: Mimulus
height: 1 to 3 feet
season: July to September

Why is this plant called monkeyflower? The common name comes from the Latin name *mimulus*, which means mimic. And you know how monkeys like to mimic, or copy, things. Hummingbirds and sphinx moths are attracted to the pink, rose, or red flowers. Look closely to see the little freckles on the lower petal.

Camas

other name: Quamash
height: 12 to 20 inches
season: April to June

Chamas is a Nootka Indian word meaning sweet. Indians depended on this nourishing plant and collected the bulbs each autumn. They baked the bulbs and ground them into flour to make flat cakes. The Chief Joseph War began when the hungry Nez Perce left their reservation in eastern Oregon to collect camas for the coming winter.

Dodecathlon dentatum

Mimulus lewisii

Camassia quamash

Elephant Head

other name: Little Red Elephant
height: 6 to 30 inches
season: June to August

Each tiny flower looks like a pink elephant with its trunk raised to trumpet a greeting. The blossoms cluster close together around the stalk. Elk think this is a tasty treat in early summer.

Pedicularis groenlandica

Stinging Nettle

other names: none
height: 2 to 6 feet
season: May to July

Ouch! Like syringes, the tiny needles under each leaf poke your skin and inject a stinging juice. (The sting goes away after awhile.) As with most nettles, the young, tender plants are edible and high in protein. Cooking the plant eliminates the sting, but wear gloves to pick it. The Latin name *urtica* comes from *uro,* meaning "to burn."

Urtica dioica

Sticky Geranium

other name: Crane's Bill
height: 1 to 3 feet
season: May to August

Geranium is Greek for crane, and the fruit of this plant looks like the beak of a crane. If a fruit pod is ripe and still closed, touch it gently and watch the tiny cups fling seeds through the air.

Geranium viscosissimum

Mountain Meadows

Mountain meadows lie under snow much of the winter, are awash with snowmelt and rain in the spring and early summer, and often dry out completely in late summer and autumn. Flowers that grow here must be able to blossom and produce seeds quickly. Then they must wait patiently until the next spring warms their home and they can grow again.

Explorer's Gentian

other name: Mountain Gentian
height: 2 to 12 inches
season: July to October

These intensely blue blossoms close at night or when it rains — maybe the blossom dislikes water in its cup. Indians and settlers used the roots of the gentian to make a tea to treat indigestion and other ailments.

Gentiana calycosa

Partridge Foot

other name: Meadow Spiraea
height: 4 to 6 inches
season: June to August

Early settlers mistakenly called the grouse a partridge. The leaves of this plant look feathery like a grouse's leg and are divided into threes, like the footprint of a grouse. Yellow centers brighten the clusters of white flowers atop each stem.

Luetkea pectinata

Western Pasque Flower

other names: Mountain Pasque Flower, Old Man of the Mountain
height: 8 to 24 inches
season: May to September

In milder climates this flower blooms around Easter. Hence the name pasque flower, since *pasque* is a derivative of the French word for Easter. The long silver hairs of the seed head make it look like a furry little creature with hair in its eyes.

Anemone occidentalis

Harebell

other names: Bluebell, Bellflower
height: 4 to 40 inches
season: June to September

Blue, lavender, or white blossoms nod gently atop slender stems. The Latin word *campanula* means little bell. Harebells often are the last flowers still blooming after hard autumn frosts wipe out other species.

Campanula rotundifolia

Paintbrush

other name: Indian Paintbrush
height: 1 to 2 feet
season: July to September

Look for the narrow, pale-green flowers hidden among the brightly colored bracts. The bracts, which look a bit like petals, range in color from magenta to yellow to orange to crimson. The roots of a paintbrush can burrow into the roots of another plant and steal part of its food. Because of that ability, the paintbrush is called a root parasite.

Castilleja spp.

Douglas' Iris

other names: Blue Flag,
    Mountain Iris
height: 6 to 30 inches
season: April to June

Iris was the Greek goddess of the rainbow. In the center of the petals, a rainbow of colors appears. The three petals symbolize faith, wisdom, and courage, and a carved iris was often placed at the top of a queen's or king's scepter.

Iris douglasiana

Mountain Forests

Mountain forests contain many different kinds of trees and shrubs. Some wildflowers live in areas that provide dense shade and shelter, while other flowers prefer the open forest floor. Streams gurgle, birds call and sing, and animals find food and shelter. Listen for the creak of two trees rubbing against each other, and watch for squirrels dashing up and down their tree homes.

Sour Grass

other names: Oxalis, Shamrock, Redwood Sorrel
height: 3 to 10 inches
season: April to September

Tiny white or pink blossoms rise above heart-shaped, clover-like leaves. Sour grass leaves have a pleasantly tart taste. The leaves are sensitive to cold and heat, and often droop on chilly nights or when the sun shines directly on them.

Oxalis oregana

Wild Ginger

other name: Snakeroot
height: 6 to 12 inches
season: April to July

You have to be very observant to spot a shy wild ginger blossom with its long, tapered, petal-like bracts. The heart-shaped leaves are shiny, and the brownish flower lies close to the ground, where it's easy to attract such pollinators as millipedes, gnats, and flies.

Asarum caudatum

Twinflower

other name: Linnaeus' Flower
height: 2 to 4 inches
season: June to September

Twin bell-shaped flowers droop at the top of the stem, and the leaves are a shiny green. The Latin name *Linnaea* comes from Linnaeus, the name of one of the world's greatest naturalists. The scientific names we use for plants today are based on his method of classifying plants.

Linnaea borealis

Western Columbine

other names: Red Columbine,
    Rock Bells
height: 1 to 3 feet
season: April to August

Hummingbirds use their long beaks to sample the nectar of columbines, but short, stubby bumblebees must drill holes in the spurs to get at the sweet prize. Columbine comes from the Latin word *columba,* which means dove. Can you see the five doves with their shared wings outspread?

Aquilegia formosa

Pacific Starflower

other names: Western Starflower,
    Indian Potato
height: 4 to 10 inches
season: April to July

Flat pink or white starburst-shaped flowers bloom in the center of a whorl of oval leaves. Indians used the juice as an eyewash, and they may have eaten the root.

Trientalis latifolia

Yellow Violet

other names: Johnny Jump-up,
    Stream Violet, Pioneer
    Violet
height: 2 to 12 inches
season: March to July

How odd! It seems like a violet should be violet, not yellow. But there are more than 300 species of violets in the world, and they come in many colors. A small pouch behind the lower petal has little pathfinders on the landing platform to direct bees to the nectar. The leaves are high in vitamin C, and the blossoms can be made into candy, jelly, syrup, or tea.

Viola glabella

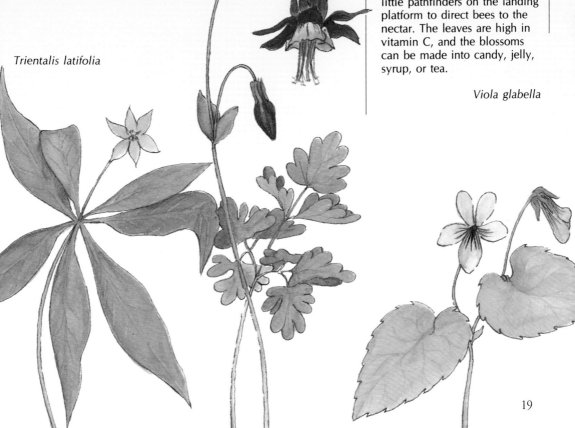

Columbia Lily

other names: Tiger Lily,
    Oregon Lily
height: 2 to 4 feet
season: June and July

This lily is named for Oregon's Columbia River. Drooping blossoms vary from lemon yellow to deep red. Orange stamens dangle downward, while the spotted petals curve up to the sky. Columbia lilies brighten many forests and roadways throughout the state.

Oregon Fawn Lily

other names: Adder's Tongue,
    Glacier Lily, Dogtooth Violet
height: 4 to 15 inches
season: March to May

Two large spotted leaves stand upright like a curious fawn with its ears perked. The pale pink or white petal tips have a little twist at the ends. Lilies are edible, and bears especially like them in spring. Lilies were the sacred flower of motherhood to the ancient Greeks and Romans.

*Erythronium
oregonum*

Yellow Lady's Slipper

other names: Noah's Ark,
    Whippoorwill Shoes
height: 12 to 18 inches
season: May and June

The brilliant yellow lip petal forms a tiny ballet slipper complete with long, striped purple petals ready to tie around a tiny ankle. Bees are good at retrieving the nectar, but other insects get trapped inside by the curled lower lip. This is a very rare orchid in Oregon—you're lucky to see one.

*Cypripedium
calceolus*

*Lilium
columbianum*

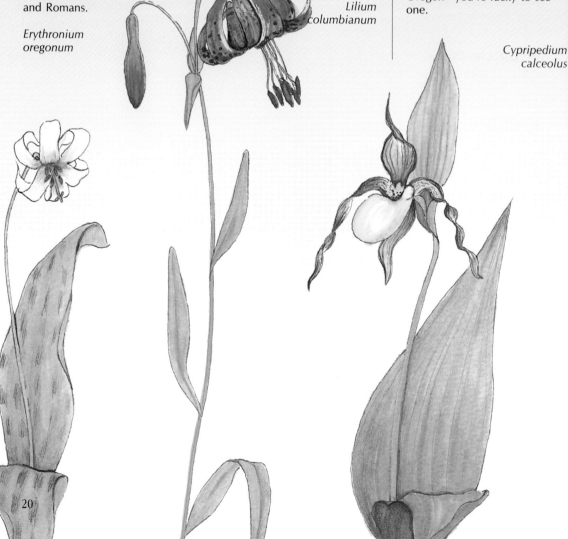

Sugarstick

other name: Candystick
height: 4 to 16 inches
season: May to August

Sugarstick is a saprophyte; it can't produce chlorophyll and must get its nourishment from the decaying matter on the forest floor. Tiny scarlet flowers hide under the white leaflike scales, and the red-and-white-striped stems look like sugary candy canes.

Allotropa virgata

Prince's Pine

other names: Pipsissewa,
    Wintergreen, Waxflower
height: 2 to 12 inches
season: June to August

Waxy pink flowers with protruding green ovaries decorate the fragile stems of this evergreen plant. The Indian word *pipisisikweu* means "it breaks into small pieces," referring to the medicinal use of prince's pine leaves to break up kidney stones.

Chimaphila umbellata

Calypso Orchid

other names: Fairyslipper, Venus-
    slipper, Deer-head Orchid
height: up to 8 inches
season: March to July

Look for this exotic flower in the deep shade of the forest. A yellow beard of hairs is enclosed by the pink or purple petals. The lip petal has orange or purplish freckles and stripes. Kalypso was a shy sea nymph in Greek mythology. Do you think she wore these flowers as slippers?

Calypso bulbosa

Devil's Club

other names: Echinopanax, Fatsia
height: 3 to 10 feet
season: June to August

The extremely sharp stem spines of the devil's club get very thick at the top, giving the spines a clublike appearance. Scratches from these spines can get very sore. In springtime, the plant's creamy flowers rise above large emerald-green leaves, followed by pretty berries that change from yellow to orange to bright red by midsummer.

Oplopanex horridum

Dutchman's Breeches

other name: Blue Staggers
height: 8 to 16 inches
season: March to June

Two puffy spurs joined at the bottom look like an old-fashioned pair of britches hanging upside-down on a clothesline. The other common name refers to the behavior of cattle if they eat this toxic plant.

Dicentra cucullaria

Beargrass

other names: Indian Basketgrass,
Squawgrass, Elkgrass,
Turkey Beard, Bear Lily,
Pine Lily
height: 2 to 5 feet
season: June to September

This plant is so popular it's amazing any are left. When bears emerge from hibernation, they like to eat the tender, juicy base of the grasslike leaves. Elk eat the flowers, stalks, and seedpods. Mountain goats eat beargrass in winter. Indians bleached the leaves and wove them to make clothing and baskets and florists use the leaves in flower arrangements.

*Xerophyllum
tenax*

Larkspur

other name: Poison
Delphinium
height: 3 to 6 feet
season: April to July

The spur at the base of each blossom is like the long hind claw on a lark's foot. Before opening, the flower bud looks like a miniature dolphin; hence the name *delphinium*, Greek for dolphin. Cattle ranchers dislike this plant because of its toxicity.

*Delphinium
trolliifolium*

Trillium

other names: Wake Robin,
Birthroot
height: 4 to 24 inches
season: March to May

"Tri" means three, as in triangle, which has three sides. Trillium has three large green leaves, three white petals that turn pinkish with age, three sepals, three styles, and three reddish berries. Trillium has the common name wake robin because it blooms early in spring—about when the first robins arrive. If you pick the bloom from a trillium, the plant may die or not bloom again for years.

*Trillium
ovatum*

Great Basin

Dry desert conditions occur in one-fourth of Oregon, mostly in the southeastern corner of the state. Not many plants can survive the harsh sun and drying winds here, but those that can have adapted in many ways. Look for tiny, delicate wildflowers; bright, showy cacti blossoms; spiny shrubs; and hardy trees. These plants show off their colorful finery at different times of the year.

Many desert flowers are annuals, growing each year from a seed into a beautiful flower in just a few weeks. They don't even try to endure the blistering heat or freezing cold of the different seasons. They just let their tough seeds lie dormant until a gentle rain awakens the life in them. Sometimes seeds have to wait several years before conditions are right. Then they quickly germinate, grow, blossom, and produce more seeds.

Rose

other name: Woods Rose
height: 3 feet
season: May to July

Rose bushes provide food and cover for wildlife such as pheasants, grouse, quail, and black bears. People like the rosehips, the plant's small pinkish fruits. Rosehips are so high in vitamin C that we use them to make vitamin tablets.

Rosa woodsii

Yellow Bell

other name: Yellow Fritillary
height: 4 to 6 inches
season: March to June

Black bears, deer, pocket gophers, and ground squirrels like to dig and eat the corms of yellow bells. People can eat them, too. The raw corm tastes like a potato, and cooked corms taste more like rice. The shy, drooping, yellow bell-shaped flower fades to a purplish color with age.

Fritillaria pudica

Mariposa Lily

other name: Sagebrush Mariposa Tulip
height: 8 to 20 inches
season: May to August

Mariposa is the Spanish word for butterfly. You can easily imagine the delicate petals as the wings of a butterfly. The lilac flowers have a maroon spot and golden fringe near the base of the three petals. Mariposa lily bulbs were an important food source for Indians and early settlers.

Calochortus macrocarpus

Blanketflower

other names: Firewheel, Indian Blanket
height: 12 to 18 inches
season: May to July

This bright flower can blanket a field in showy colors. Individually, each blossom is like a fiery pinwheel. Look closely at the blossom, called a composite: the brightly colored pinwheel parts are called ray flowers, and the center disk is composed of dozens of tightly packed, individual florets.

Wallflower

other name: Prairie Rocket
height: 1 to 3 feet
season: June to August

In Europe, this plant often grows in the rocky soil along old walls hence the name wallflower. In Oregon, you're more likely to see it in the dry grasslands. The blossoms may be bright yellow, orange, or a dark burnt-orange color. Pikas and rock-chucks feast on the leaves and stems.

Erysimum capitatum

Steershead

other name: Squirrelcorn
height: 2 to 4 inches
season: June and July

Two inner petals form a long nose, while the outer two petals curve upward like the horns on a miniature steer's head. This tiny, low-growing flower blooms among the sagebrush. Although it looks like a cow's head, steers and other livestock must avoid this poisonous plant.

Dicentra uniflora

Woolly Marbles

other name: Woolly-heads
height: 1 to 2 inches
season: April to July

Woolly silver marbles are cupped in a bowl of green leaves, and it's fun to gently touch the furry little flowers.

Psilocarphus oregonus

Gaillardia pulchella

25

Shrubs and Berries

Many plants produce berries after their flowers have been fertilized. Some berries are delicious, while others are poisonous. Never eat a berry if you aren't sure it's safe!

The soft pulp of a berry provides protection and nourishment for the seed enclosed within. Birds and animals eat the berries, leaves, stems, and even roots. People also use many parts of berry plants for food, medicines, and dyes. No wonder so many berry bushes have thorns! They need some protection against overuse.

Strawberry

other names: none
height: 3 to 4 inches
season: May to July

Note where you see the pretty, white, five-petaled blossoms so you can return later to savor the sweet wild strawberries. Yum! Birds, turtles, small rodents, and bears also enjoy eating them. This plant got its name because many people lay straw under their garden strawberries to keep them from rotting on wet ground.

Fragaria virginiana

Blackberry

other names: none
height: up to 9 feet
season: June to September

Blackberries grow in thickets, like the dense brambles in *Sleeping Beauty*. These berries are good to eat either fresh or dried. Many people enjoy a cup of tea brewed from blackberry leaves, and the roots are used in some medicines. What a useful plant!

Rubus ursinus

Salal

other names: none
height: 4 inches to 4 feet
season: May to July

Salal berries are an important food for wildlife. People often use the leaves in floral arrangements. Some folks brew tea from the menthol-tasting leaves and nibble on the berries. The berries are delicious when gathered on the coast, where ocean spray coats them with tangy salt.

Gualtheria shallon

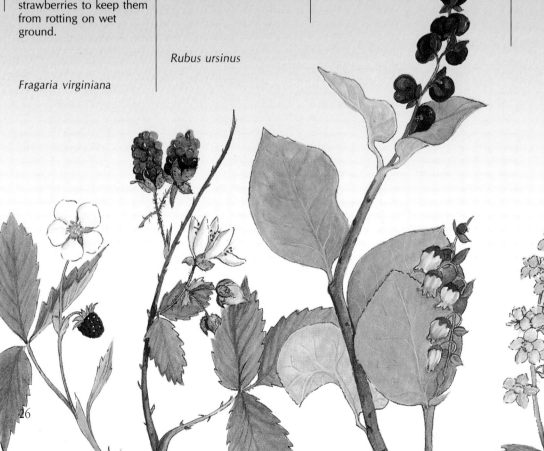

Oregon Grape

other names: Mahonia, Barberry,
Holly Grape
height: 4 to 12 inches
season: March to June

In 1899, the Portland
Women's Club chose the tall
Oregon grape to be the state
flower. In springtime, bright
yellow blossoms cluster on the
stems. The sour, bluish berries
are edible, and some of the
hollylike leaves turn deep red in
autumn. Indians made a yellow
clothing dye from the bark, and
it has many useful medicinal
qualities. What a good choice
for a state flower!

Mahonia aquifolium

Kinnikinnick

other names: Bearberry, Mat or
Low-growing Manzanita
height: 3 to 6 inches
season: May to June

Kinnikinnick is an Algonquin
Indian word for mixed, because
Indians mixed the leaves with
other plants to make pipe
tobacco. When cooked slowly,
the bland berries pop like
popcorn. Deer and bighorn
sheep browse on the leaves
and twigs in winter, and
songbirds, turkeys, grouse,
rodents, and bears eat the
berries. Some people use the
leaves to make a medicinal tea.

*Arctostaphylos
uva-ursi*

Huckleberry

other name: Wild Blueberry
height: 6 to 24 inches
season: June and July

Huckleberries are one of
the best-tasting berries in
the world. Animals think
so, too. Huckleberries are
a staple food for black
bears, grouse, ptarmigans,
rodents, martens, and
coyotes. Many other birds
and mammals eat them,
too. Look for reddish
huckleberries in the forests
at low elevations and
bluish-purple berries
higher in the mountains.

*Vaccinium
ovatum*

27

Conclusion

"Over here! Look at me!" shout the bright colors of a wildflower. The showy blossom attracts us, but more importantly, it attracts insects and other flying and crawling visitors that pollinate it. Bees, moths, beetles, butterflies, hummingbirds, and even ants and bats are essential for wildflowers to make seeds.

So when you bend down to enjoy the sweet smell of a fresh blossom, remember to share the space with other creatures. Wildflowers may like us to look at them, but they depend on their other visitors for survival.

Glossary

Alternate	Not opposite each other
Annual	A plant that lives for one season
Anther	The part of the stamen containing pollen
Berry	A fleshy fruit containing seeds
Biennial	A plant that lives for two years
Bract	Leaflike scales
Bulb	A plant bud usually below the ground
Corm	A bulblike underground swelling of a stem
Composite	Flower heads composed of clusters of ray and disk flowers
Disk flower	Tubular florets in the center part of a composite flower head
Evergreen	Bearing green leaves throughout the year
Filament	The stalk of the stamen
Floret	A small flower that is part of a cluster
Flower	Part of a plant containing male and/or female reproductive parts
Flower head	A dense cluster of flowers atop a stem
Fruit	A seed-bearing part of a plant
Habitat	The community where a plant naturally grows
Head	A dense cluster of flowers atop a stem
Herb	A seed plant with no woody tissue, whose stems die back to the ground each year
Irregular	Nonsymmetrical in shape
Nectar	Sweet liquid produced by flowers to attract insects
Opposite	Pairs of leaves opposite each other on a stem
Ovary	The part of the pistil that contains the developing seeds
Parasitic	Growing on and deriving nourishment from another plant
Pathfinders	Lines that guide insects to the nectar
Pedicel	The supporting stem of a single flower
Perennial	A plant that lives from year to year

Petals	Floral leaves inside the sepals that attract pollinators
Petiole	The stem supporting a leaf
Pistil	The seed-bearing organ of a flower
Pollen	Powder-like cells produced by the stamens
Ray flower	The flowers around the edge of a flower head; each flower may resemble a single petal
Regular	Alike in size and shape
Rhizome	Underground stem or rootstock
Saprophyte	A plant that lives on dead organic matter
Seed	Developed female egg
Seedpod	Sack enclosing the developed female egg(s)
Sepal	The outermost floral leaf that protects the delicate petals
Shrub	Low woody plant, usually having several stems
Spadix	Fleshy spike that bears flowers
Spathe	Leafy covering connected to the base of a spadix
Spur	Hollow appendage of a petal or sepal
Stamen	Pollen-producing organ of a flower
Stigma	The end of the pistil that collects pollen
Style	The slender stalk of a pistil
Succulent	A plant with thick, fleshy leaves or stems that conserve moisture
Tendril	Slender, twining extension of a leaf or stem
Tuber	A thickened underground stem having numerous buds
Whorl	Three or more leaves or branches growing from a common point

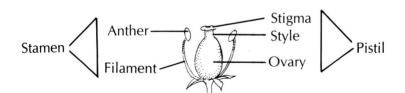

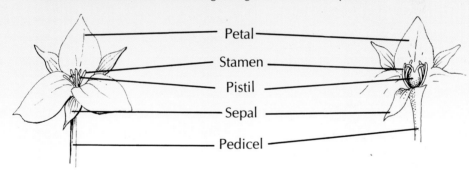

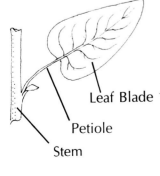

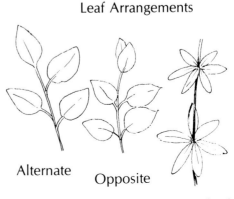

Leaf Arrangements

Leaf Blade

Petiole

Stem

Alternate   Opposite

Whorl

Where to See Wildflowers

Wildflowers can be found anywhere in Oregon, but some of the best places are state and federal parks, forests, refuges, and recreation areas. Many of these areas have campgrounds, picnic areas, nature trails, and interpretive services to help visitors see and appreciate these lands and their wildflowers. You can get information about these areas by contacting the following organizations:

Oneonta Gorge
Multnomah Falls
Horsetail Falls
McCord Creek
Tom McCall Preserve
Eagle Creek
Columbia River Gorge
   National Scenic Area
Waucoma Center, Suite 200
902 Wasco Avenue
Hood River, OR 97031
(503) 386-2333

Cape Falcon State Park
Saddle Mountain State Park
Mary S. Young State Park
Tryon State Park
Oregon State Parks
525 Trade Street SE #301
Salem, OR 97310
(503) 378-6305

Cape Perpetua Visitor Center
P.O. Box 274
Yachats, OR 97498
(503) 547-3289

National Forests in Oregon
Pacific Northwest Region
319 SW Pine Street (P.O. Box 3623)
Portland OR 97208
(503) 221-2877

Oregon Dunes National Recreation Area
855 Highway Avenue
Reedsport, OR 97467
(503) 271-3611

Leach Botanical Garden
6704 SE 122nd
Portland, OR 97266
(503) 761-9503
also in Portland:
Hoyt Arboretum in Forest Park
Berry Botanical Garden
Powell Butte Park

Mount Pisgah Arboretum, Eugene

Frenchglen Wayside,
   near Malheur Wildlife Refuge

Crater Lake National Park
P.O. Box 7
Crater Lake, OR 97604
(503)594-2211

Hells Canyon National Recreation Area
P.O. Box 490
Enterprise, OR 97828
(503) 426-3151

National Wildlife Refuges in Oregon
Lloyd 500 Building, Suite 1692
500 NE Multnomah Street
Portland, OR 97232
(503) 231-6168

Index